ONE HUNDRED WAYS
TO
Friendship

ONE HUNDRED WAYS
TO
Friendship

COMPILED BY

Celia Haddon

Hodder & Stoughton
LONDON SYDNEY AUCKLAND

British Library Cataloguing in Publication Data
A record for this book is available from
the British Library

ISBN 0 340 78558 6

Printed and bound in Great Britain
by Clays Ltd, St Ives plc

Hodder and Stoughton
A Division of Hodder Headline Ltd
338 Euston Road
London NW1 3BH

Contents

Celebrating Friendship

It is a good thing to be rich, and a good thing to be strong, but it is a better thing to be beloved of many friends.

EURIPIDES,
Greek playwright, 480–406 BC

Friends are patient and kind,
They are not jealous or boastful,
They are not arrogant or rude.
Friends do not insist on having their
    own way,
They are not irritable or resentful,
They do not rejoice at wrong,
But delight in what is right.
Friendship bears all things, believes
    all things, hopes all things,
      endures all things.

ADAPTED FROM 1 CORINTHIANS 13

Friendship is a serious affection; the most sublime of all affections, because it is founded on principle, and cemented by time.

MARY WOLLSTONECRAFT,
feminist, 1759–97

Friendship is a calm and sedate affection, conducted by reason and cemented by habit; springing from long acquaintance and mutual obligations, without jealousies or fears.

DAVID HUME,
philosopher, 1711–76

Friends are the family we choose for ourselves.

PROVERB

We are most of us very lonely in this world; you who have any who love you, cling to them and thank God.

WILLIAM MAKEPEACE THACKERAY, novelist, 1811–63

Life is to be fortified with many friendships. To love and be loved is the greatest happiness of existence.

SYDNEY SMITH,
clergyman and wit, 1771–1845

It is the secret sympathy,
The silver link, the silken tie,
Which heart to heart, and mind to
    mind
In body and in soul can bind.

SIR WALTER SCOTT,
novelist and poet, 1771–1832

F riends are the bacon
bits in the salad bowl
of life.

AUTHOR UNKNOWN

Happiness does not depend on money, or leisure, or society, or even on health; it depends on our relation to those we love.

ROBERT SOUTHEY,
poet, 1774–1843

So long as we love, we serve. So long as we are loved by others I would almost say we are indispensable; and no man is useless while he has a friend.

ROBERT LOUIS STEVENSON,
writer, 1850–94

The feeling of friendship is like that of being comfortably filled with roast beef ...

SAMUEL JOHNSON,
essayist, 1709–84

Wherever you are, it is your own
friends who make your world.

WILLIAM JAMES,
philosopher, 1842–1910

Ah, how good it feels,
The hand of an old friend!

HENRY WADSWORTH LONGFELLOW,
poet, 1807–82

The mind never unbends itself so agreeably as in the conversation of a well-chosen friend.

JOSEPH ADDISON,
essayist, 1672–1719

He that is thy friend indeed,
He will help thee in thy need!
If thou sorrow, he will weep!
If thou wake, he cannot sleep!
Thus, of every grief in heart,
He with thee doth bear a part!
These are certain signs to know
Faithful friend from flatt'ring foe.

RICHARD BARNFIELD,
poet, 1574–1627

The reward of friendship is itself. The man who hopes for anything else does not understand what true friendship is.

ST AILRED OF RIEVAULX, historian, 1109–66

Making New Friends

Blessed are they who have the gift of making friends, for it is one of God's best gifts. It involves many things, but, above all, the power of going out of one's self, and appreciating whatever is noble and loving in another.

THOMAS HUGHES,
novelist, 1822–96

The only reward of virtue is virtue; the only way to have a friend is to be one.

RALPH WALDO EMERSON,
essayist, 1803–82

We cannot tell the precise moment when friendship is formed. As in filling a vessel drop by drop, there is at last a drop which makes it run over; so in a series of kindnesses there is at last one which makes the heart run over.

JAMES BOSWELL,
biographer, 1740–95

Madam, I have been looking for a person who disliked gravy all my life; let us swear eternal friendship.

SYDNEY SMITH,
clergyman and wit, 1771–1845

23

I want someone to laugh with me, someone to be grave with me, someone to please me and help my discrimination with his or her own remark, and at times, no doubt, to admire my acuteness and penetration.

ROBERT BURNS,
poet, 1759–96

Perhaps the most delightful friendships are those in which there is much agreement, much disputation and yet more personal liking.

GEORGE ELIOT,
novelist, 1819–80

For binding friendships, a similarity of manners is the surest tie.

PLINY THE YOUNGER,
Roman writer, 62–114

The covetous, the angry, the proud, the jealous, the talkative, cannot but make ill friends, as well as the false.

WILLIAM PENN,
Quaker, 1644–1718

Sweet language will multiply friends:
and a fair-speaking tongue will
increase kind greetings.

ECCLESIASTICUS

If thou wouldest get a friend, prove him first, and be not hasty to credit him.

For some man is a friend for his own occasion, and will not abide in the day of thy trouble.

And there is a friend, who being turned to enmity and strife will discover thy reproach.

Again, some friend is a companion at the table, and will not continue in the day of thy affliction.

But in thy prosperity he will be as thyself, and will be bold over thy servants.

If thou be brought low, he will be
against thee, and will hide himself
from thy face.

ECCLESIASTICUS.

From wine what sudden friend-ship springs!

JOHN GAY,
poet, 1683–1732

Do not be hasty in forming friendships, but do not break off those you have formed.

SOLON,
Athenian lawgiver, 638–559 BC

Friendship ... may be of the shallowest kind and yet the friendship be of the truest. For all the different traits of our nature must get their airing through friends, the trivial as well as the significant ... Each friend calls out some particular trait in us.

RANDOLPH BOURNE,
writer, 1886–1918

Be a friend to thyself, and
others will befriend thee.

PROVERB

Take care thou be not made a fool by flatterers, for even the wisest men are abused by these ... It is hard to know them from friends, they are so obsequious and full of protestations; for as a wolf resembles a dog, so doth a flatterer a friend.

SIR WALTER RALEIGH,
writer and explorer, 1552–1618

 How to Treat a Friend

Life is mainly froth and bubble,
Two things stand like stone –
Kindness in another's trouble,
Courage in your own.

ADAM LINDSAY GORDON,
poet, 1833–70

G ive and take make good friends.

SCOTTISH PROVERB

We know diseases of stoppings, and suffocations, are the most dangerous in the body; and it is not much otherwise in the mind ... No receipt openeth the heart but a true friend, to whom you may impart griefs, joys, fears, hopes, suspicions, counsels, and whatsover lieth upon the heart to oppress it, in a kind of civil shrift or confession.

FRANCIS BACON,
writer and politician, 1561–1626

Everyone hears what you say.
Friends listen to what you say.
Best friends listen to what you don't
say.

AUTHOR UNKNOWN

To accept a favour from a friend
is to confer one.

JOHN CHURTON COLLINS,
critic, 1848–1908

Tis the privilege of friendship to talk nonsense, and have her nonsense respected.

CHARLES LAMB,
essayist, 1775–1834

Give up time to your friends, be at leisure to your wife, relax your mind, give rest to your body, so that you may the better fulfil your accustomed occupation.

PHAEDRUS,
Roman writer, first century AD

He who does good to his friend, does good to himself.

DESIDERIUS ERASMUS,
humanist, 1466–1536

A hedge between, keeps friendship green.

PROVERB

We should behave to our friends
as we would wish our friends
to behave to us.

ARISTOTLE,
philosopher, 384–322 BC

Don't walk before me, I may not
  follow,
Don't walk behind me, I may not
  lead.
Just walk beside me and be my
  friend.

AUTHOR UNKNOWN

Treat your friends for what you know them to be. Regard no surfaces. Consider not what they did, but what they intended.

HENRY DAVID THOREAU,
philosopher, 1817–62

I was angry with my friend;
I told my wrath, my wrath did end.
I was angry with my foe;
I told it not, my wrath did grow.

WILLIAM BLAKE,
poet, artist and mystic, 1757–1827

When therefore it shall happen, as happen it will, that you or I have disappointed the expectation of the other, you are not to suppose that you have lost me or that I intended to lose you; nothing will remain but to repair the fault, and to go on as if it had never been committed.

SAMUEL JOHNSON,
essayist, 1709–84

A friend should bear his friend's infirmities.

WILLIAM SHAKESPEARE,
playwright, 1564–1616

My friend, keep well thy tongue, and keep thy friend.

GEOFFREY CHAUCER,
poet, 1345–1400

A slender acquaintance with the world must convince every man, that actions, not words, are the true criterion of the attachment of friends; and that the most liberal professions of good will are very far from being the surest marks of it.

GEORGE WASHINGTON,
American president, 1732–99

How not to Treat a Friend

Few things tend more to alienate friendship than a want of punctuality in our engagements. I have known the breach of a promise to dine or sup to break up more than one intimacy.

WILLIAM HAZLITT,
essayist, 1778–1830

The chain of friendship, however bright, does not stand the attrition of constant close contact.

SIR WALTER SCOTT,
novelist and poet, 1771–1832

Angry friendship is sometimes as bad as calm enmity.

EDMUND BURKE,
political philosopher, 1729–97

Give me the avowed, erect and
    manly foe;
Firm I can meet, perhaps return the
    blow;
But of all plagues, good heaven, thy
    wrath can send,
Save me, oh, save me from the
    candid friend.

GEORGE CANNING,
politician and writer, 1770–1827

Few friendships would survive if each man knew what his friend says about him when he is not there, even though it is said sincerely and dispassionately.

BLAISE PASCAL,
theologian and mathematician,
1623–62

The man that hails you Tom or Jack,
And proves by thumps upon your
   back
How he esteems your merit,
Is such a friend, that one had need
Be very much his friend indeed
To pardon or to bear it.

WILLIAM COWPER,
poet, 1731–1800

It is always safe to learn, even from our enemies – seldom safe to venture to instruct, even our friends.

CHARLES CALEB COLTON,
clergyman and sportsman, 1780–1832

The holy passion of friendship is of so sweet and steady and loyal and enduring a nature that it will last through a whole lifetime, if not asked to lend money.

MARK TWAIN,
writer, 1835–1910

Words beget anger: anger brings
    forth blows;
Blows make of dearest friends
    immortal foes …
Far better 'twere for either to be mute
Than for to murder friendship, by
    dispute.

ROBERT HERRICK,
poet, 1591–1674

A dispute begun in jest upon a subject which a moment before was on both parts regarded with careless indifference, is continued by the desire of conquest, till vanity kindles into rage, and opposition rankles into enmity. Against this hasty mischief I know not what security can be obtained: men will be sometimes surprised into quarrels.

SAMUEL JOHNSON,
essayist, 1709–84

He that gives advice to his friend and exacts obedience to it, does not the kindness and ingenuity of a friend, but the office and pertness of a schoolmaster.

JEREMY TAYLOR,
theologian, 1613–67

Unkindness in words or actions among friends affects us at the first instant in the inmost recesses of our souls.

RICHARD STEELE,
essayist and playwright, 1672–1729

It's a poor friendship that needs to be constantly bought.

PROVERB

It is more shameful to distrust one's friends than to be deceived by them.

FRANÇOIS, DUC DE LA
ROCHFOUCAULD,
writer, 1613–80

Keeping Old Friends

Old friends are the great blessing of one's later years – half a word conveys one's meaning. They have memory of the same events and have the same mode of thinking.

HORACE WALPOLE,
man of letters, 1717–97

Make new friends, but keep the old;
One is silver, the other gold.

AUTHOR UNKNOWN

Think when you are enraged with anyone, what would probably become your sentiments should he die during the dispute.

WILLIAM SHENSTONE,
poet and gardener, 1714–63

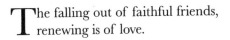

The falling out of faithful friends,
renewing is of love.

RICHARD EDWARDS,
playwright and choirmaster, 1523–66

It should be part of our private ritual to devote a quarter of an hour every day to the enumeration of the good qualities of our friends. When we are not *active*, we fall back idly upon defects, even of those whom we most love.

MARK RUTHERFORD,
writer, 1831–1913

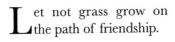

L et not grass grow on
the path of friendship.

NATIVE AMERICAN PROVERB

Old friends burn dim, like lamps in
  noisesome air;
Love them for what they are; nor
  love them less,
Because to thee they are not what
  they were.

SAMUEL TAYLOR COLERIDGE,
  poet, 1772–1834

Friendship is the great chain of human society, and intercourse of letters is one of the chiefest links of that chain.

JAMES HOWELL,
writer, 1593–1666

A friend once won need never be lost, if we will be only trusty and true ourselves. Friends may part, not merely in body, but in spirit for a while. In the bustle of business and the accidents of life, they may lose sight of each other for years; and more, they may begin to differ in their success in life, in their opinions, in their habits, and there may be, for a time, coldness and estrangement between them, but not for ever if each will be trusty and true.

CHARLES KINGSLEY,
novelist, 1819–75

Let us conclude by saying to you, what I have had on too frequent occasions to say to my other remaining old friends, the fewer we become, the more let us love one another.

BENJAMIN FRANKLIN,
scientist and statesman, 1706–90

My friendships are increased by new ones, yet no part of the warmth I felt for the old is diminished.

ALEXANDER POPE,
poet, 1688–1744

Are new friends who are worthy of friendship, to be preferred to old friends? The question is unworthy of a human being, for there should be no surfeit of friendships as there is of other things; and, as in the case of wines that improve with age, the oldest friendships ought to be the most delightful; moreover, the well-known adage is true: men must eat many a peck of salt together before the claims of friendship are fulfilled.

CICERO,
Roman orator and writer, 106–43

Old friends are best. King James used to call for his old shoes; they were easiest for his feet.

JOHN SELDEN,
historian, 1584–1654

Friendship, 'the wine of life', should, like a well-stocked cellar, be thus continually renewed; and it is consolatory to think, that although we can seldom add what will equal the generous first-growths of our youth, yet friendship becomes insensibly old in much less time than is commonly imagined, and not many years are required to make it very mellow and pleasant.

JAMES BOSWELL,
diarist, 1740–95

Those Other Friends

Animals are such agreeable friends – they ask no questions, they pass no criticisms.

GEORGE ELIOT,
novelist, 1819–80

To a Cat

Dogs may fawn on all and some
As they come;
You, a friend of loftier mind,
Answer friends alone in kind.
Just your foot upon my hand
Softly bids it understand.

ALGERNON SWINBURNE,
poet, 1837–1909

My playful cat and honest dog
Are all the friends I have.

<small>EBENEZER ELLIOTT,</small>
poet and merchant, 1781–1849

The one absolutely unselfish friend that a man can have in this selfish world, the one that never deserts him, the one that never proves ungrateful or treacherous, is his dog. He will sleep on the cold ground where the wintry winds blow and the snow drives fiercely if only he may be near his master's side. He will kiss the hand that has no food to offer.

GEORGE G. VEST,
lawyer and senator, 1830–1904

I neither care who's in or out,
Whether Tory, whether Whig,
I love my country, King and Queen,
But best of all I love my pig.

FREDERICK FORREST,
comic writer, fl. 1760s

I like cats and dogs very much indeed. What jolly chaps they are! They are much superior to human beings as companions. They do not quarrel or argue with you. They never talk about themselves, but listen to you while you talk about yourself, and keep up an appearance of being interested in the conversation. They never say unkind things. They never tell us of our own faults 'merely for our own good' . . . They are always glad to see us.

JEROME K. JEROME,
writer, 1859–1927

No one who has carefully and kindly brought up a kitten from its birth, could fail to find it first a charming playmate and then a firm friend.

GERTRUDE JEKYLL,
garden designer, 1843–1932

With eye upraised his master's look
    to scan,
The joy, the solace, and the aid of
    man;
The rich man's guardian and the
    poor man's friend,
The only creature faithful to the end.

AUTHOR UNKNOWN

If it be the chief point of friendship to comply with a friend's motions and inclinations [my dog] possesses this in an eminent degree; he lies down when I sit, and walks where I walk, which is more than many good friends can pretend to . . . Histories are more full of examples of the fidelity of dogs than of friends.

ALEXANDER POPE,
poet, 1688–1744

It often happens that a man is more humanely related to a cat or dog than to any human being.

HENRY DAVID THOREAU,
philosopher, 1817–62

A cat . . . shares your hours of work, of solitude, of melancholy. He spends whole evenings on your knee, purring and dozing, content with your silence, and spurning for your sake the society of his kind.

THÉOPHILE GAUTIER,
poet and novelist, 1811–72

The great pleasure of a dog is that you may make a fool of yourself with him and not only will he not scold you, but he will make a fool of himself too.

SAMUEL BUTLER,
writer and painter, 1835–1902

When I am playing with my cat, who knows whether she have more sport in dallying with me than I have in gaming with her? We entertain one another with mutual apish tricks.

MICHEL MONTAIGNE,
essayist, 1533–92

Spirituality in Friendship

Christian charity is friendship to all the world . . . The more we love, the better we are; and the greater our friendships are, the dearer we are to God. Let them be as dear, and let them be as perfect, and let them be as many as you can; there is no danger in it.

JEREMY TAYLOR,
theologian, 1613–67

The love of our private friends is the only preparatory exercise for the love of all men.

JOHN HENRY NEWMAN,
cardinal, 1801–90

Friendship's an abstract of love's
    noble flame.
'Tis love refined and purged from all
    its dross,
'Tis next to angel's love, if not the
    same,
As strong as passion is, though not so
    gross.
It antedates a glad eternity
And is a heaven in epitome.

        KATHERINE PHILIPS,
        poet, 1631–64

A friend is a gift of God and only he who made hearts can unite them.

> ROBERT SOUTHEY,
> poet, 1774–1843

F riendship is the nearest thing we know to religion. God is love and to make religion akin to friendship is simply to give it the highest expression conceivable by man.

> JOHN RUSKIN,
> art critic, 1819–1900

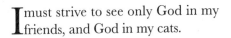

I must strive to see only God in my
friends, and God in my cats.

FLORENCE NIGHTINGALE,
nurse and social reformer,
1820–1910

It is necessary for those who seek true virtue in the world to make good and holy friendships, to encourage, help and guide one another on the path of virtue. Those who travel across a plain need not assist each other but those who travel on rough and slippery roads must cling to each other for security.

St Francis de Sales,
bishop, 1567–1622

Friendship, unlike love which is weakened by fruition, grows up, thrives, and increases by enjoyment; and being of itself spiritual, the soul is reformed by the habit of it.

MICHEL MONTAIGNE,
essayist, 1533–92

Beloved, let us love one another: for
    love is of God; and every one that
    loveth is born of God, and
    knoweth God.
He that loveth not knoweth not God;
    for God is love …
Beloved, if God so loved us, we
    ought also to love one another.
No man hath seen God at any time.
    If we love one another, God
    dwelleth in us, and his love is
    perfected in us.

EPISTLE OF ST JOHN

This is my commandment, that ye love one another, as I have loved you. Greater love hath no man than this, that a man lay down his life for his friends.

JESUS CHRIST